Desmond Morse - Boycott
1974

A PILGRIMAGE OF SONG

OTHER BOOKS BY THE AUTHOR

*General Works*
Ten Years in a London Slum
We do See Life
Fields of Yesterday
Great Crimes of the Bible
Is it a Sin?
How can I be Happy?
A Tapestry of Toil (autobiography)

*On the Anglo-Catholic Movement*
The Secret Story of the Oxford Movement
Lead, Kindly Light
They Shine Like Stars, incorporating and enlarging the above, with illustrations

*Sermons and Addresses*
"Saith The Preacher"
Mystic Glow (the Symbolism of the Cross)
A Lantern for Lent
The Pilgrim's Way
Wayside Words
Credo—A Tract for New Times
Confirmation and Communion
A Tramping Parson's Message
Seven Holy Words
Three Holy Fruits

*Theological: General*
God and Everyman
Fear Not

*For Children*
The Devout Chorister
When we are very Good
A Nursery Prayer Book
Simplicitas and His Brethren

*Periodicals*
The Angel: an Illustrated Magazine about the Song School

*Series*
Editor of The Keble Books

*Monograph*
The Boy Bishop Book, illustrated
A day in the Life of the Song School, illustrated

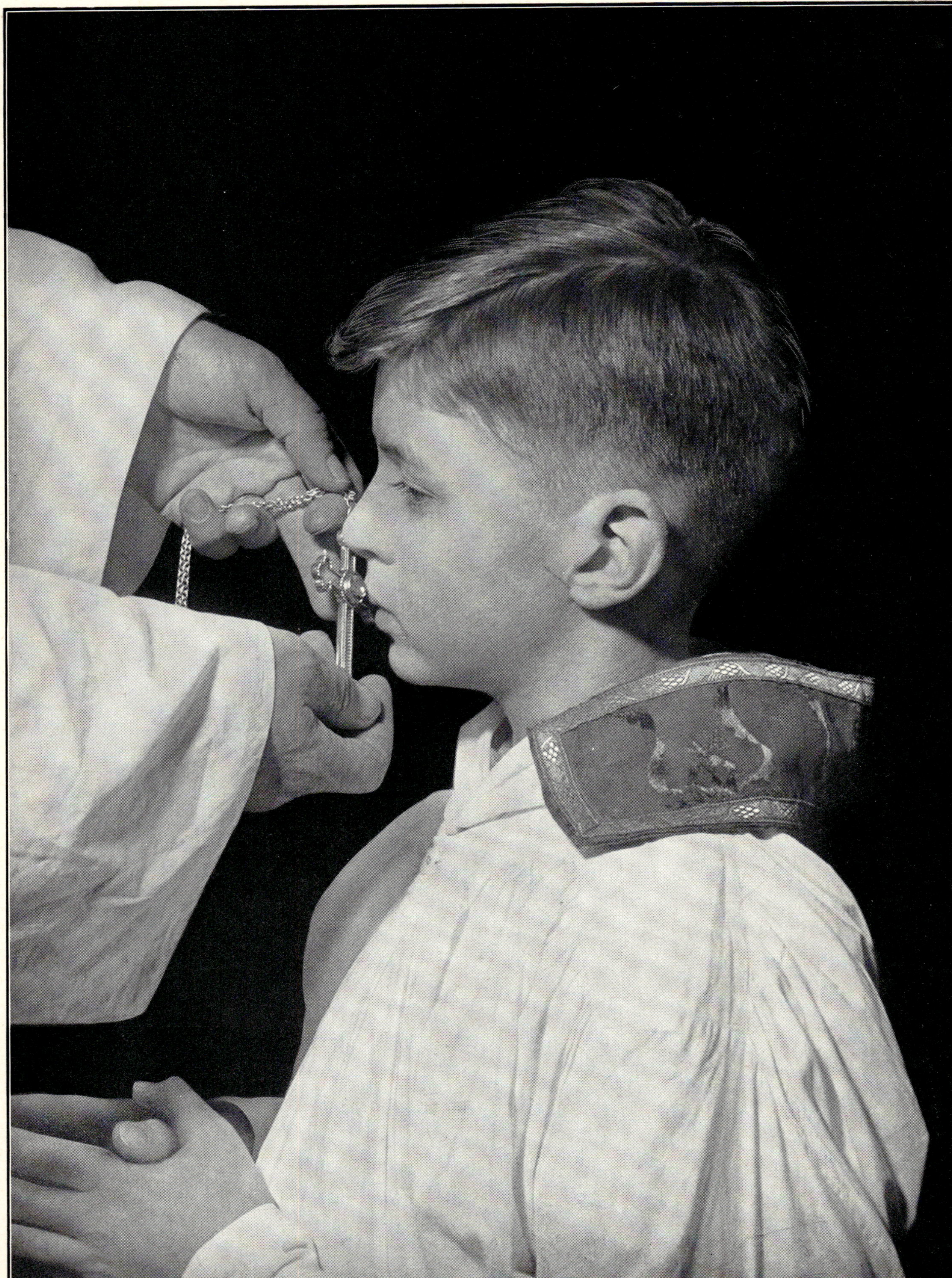

# A PILGRIMAGE OF SONG

BY THE
REVD. DESMOND MORSE-BOYCOTT

ILLUSTRATED

THE FAITH PRESS
Leighton Buzzard, Beds., LU7 7NQ

PRINTED IN GREAT BRITAIN
*in 10pt. Baskerville type*
BY THE FAITH PRESS LTD.
LEIGHTON BUZZARD
SBN 7164 0235 1

## What the Author has to say

Please to remember, or if the matter is new to you know, that St. Mary-of-the-Angels Song School was founded on the pattern of All Saints' Choir School, Margaret Street, W.1, as the Choir School for the slum parish of St. Mary's, Seymour—now Eversholt Street, Somers Town—a desolate slum area, hard-by Euston Station, wedged between Camden Town, St. Pancras and Kings Cross. I did not know as I trudged through the alley ways and by-ways of Camden Town that my family had founded it (*vide* my *Tapestry of Toil*). A Trust Deed was drawn, in 1932, to ensure parochial permanence, as we hoped, but otherwise to carry our work into the future.

In my book I have, in a modified manner, described how, to my deep distress, the Parish Church separated from the Song School, which, thrown upon itself and "out on a limb", could but throw itself upon the Church at large.

Unexpectedly, it was found by legal advisers that the Trust Deed covered its independence. The following policy was determined; not immediately but as the work developed.

a. To place itself at its own charges at the disposal of the Church at large, whether for a Service or a Society Meeting, provided that it might beg an Alms at the door, so to fulfil the vocation of "Handmaid to the Church of England".

In this respect there has never been acceptance by "the Establishment".

b. On the secular level to vie with the Vienna Song School. In quality, this was achieved, to the disapprobation of the then Board, later Ministry, of Education, which regarded Music as a subtraction from General Education and Singing Trips as exploitation of the young.

We "soldiered on."

The following is the record of a single trip. On a raw morning in March we all got up before dawn for a Noon wedding near Sherborne in Dorsetshire and in progress (with breakfast packets) saw the sunrise over Stonehenge, then pulled up at an inn, which was snug and spotless, in its old simplicity a page of English history and so on to Trent church, a gem of the Church of England, where the Rector showed us round. There was a superb recumbent marble effigy of a predecessor.

I remarked that the village honoured its Rectors. He replied drily, to the boys' amazement: "That memorial was erected by the Rector himself 25 years before he died. He was a rich man."

So on to where we had to sing the wedding: after which to the "Digby Arms" in Sherborne for a banquet which well made up for the scanty breakfast. Thence to the Minster to see the bones (*inter alia*) of two of the brothers of King Alfred. Then over to sing in an ancient Alms House to a few very old ladies.

I have enlarged upon one day's labour, worth a week in the class-room, because it was regarded by the Ministry of Education as heresy and exploitation. It earned several days' bread money.

Newman, in his *The Idea of a University,* was a century ahead of true ideas in education. He regarded a curriculum as a single instrument, not as the study of isolated subjects. "All knowledge is a whole and the separate Sciences part of one." This became luminously true in our Song School wherein all subjects were subordinate to religion, as the hub of the wheel, and every subject a shaft therefrom, enclosed by the binding circle of Music, gaining a unity in separateness. It was in the Music Room that a boy learnt, not only the artistry of Worship but the purest English; there gained by heart and with the understanding that comes from the wedding of poetry and prose with music, a treasury so stored in memory as to illuminate and reward his life-time.

But the Ministry of Education was blind to these things, being concerned with ventilation, standardization, re-organization and if possible suppression. Any School *sui generis* was anathema.

## Musick

I acknowledge the assistance of fine musicians and choir trainers over the many years, to whom I gave a free hand and scope, looking upon myself only as the creator of the instrument for them to play upon. I was jealous to see that a new-comer kept the best of his predecessor's work. We built up a treasury of School compositions. We went into films, a day here and a week there. This part of our work was fascinating and curious. Why, for instance, were we called to put our voices into the mouths of the Westminster Abbey boys in a previous Coronation in "a topical film". Similarly we had to supply the Sistine Choir of St. Peter's, Rome. I shall never know the answer. We took our fee and were thankful.

There were exacting occasions such as a week on "Tom Brown's Schooldays", when the management called me in to rescue the shooting from chaos of misbehaviour, and another on "The Lease of Life", starring Robert Donat. In the former instance the star and the Rugby boys were responsible.

Innumerable other engagements elude my pen so perhaps conclusion may be made with the "Black Knight", the theme in the time of chivalry, a quality that was lacking in our remuneration, in the event.

The Agent who engaged us for two days ("I always have your boys because of their behaviour") had briefed us well, and it was a point of honour to be fully rehearsed before setting out in the dawn hours, scantily breakfasted but hoping to augment in some café if laid on by Providence. We arrived by 8 a.m., the boys were robed as mediaeval ragamuffins and left to kick their heels for the next two hours.

The point of this reminiscence is that the Director of the Film had budgetted for the loss of the first day in rehearsing turbulent tykes, such as he was used to employing, but finding everything tailored to hand got through two days' work in one, so we received only one day's pay.

It remains only to add that when serving a church we charged only expenses and, not infrequently, spent a penny for three farthings. The emphasis was on service. If only the Church of England (a hard Mother towards any child unsuckled at her Establishment breasts) had given us recognition as her Musical Handmaid, we could have brightened formal occasions, such as the deadly-dull Society Annuals. The nearest we came to it was when we gave a musical acclaim to the exiled Emperor of Ethiopia, who in his delight gave us gold rings, and to the Patriarch of Rumania, who gave us £100 with his blessing. No Bishop cared for us. Being "extra Diocesan" we were "nobody's child". And, of course, there was the Royal School of Church Music, with which we were never in competition because its work was centripetal (relating choirs to itself) but ours centrifugal, going out to inspire local choirs where they belonged.

Why were we left out from the City Guild church distribution? That would have given us status, a platform and means of finance.

## Meaners

Without any doubt the adoption of the Eton suit for Sunday and ceremonial wear and the blue-and-badged smock or blue-coat were conducive to good manners. The former, introduced in pre-Choir School days, excited no opposition except, of course, from the boy population of Somers Town. The boy had a new and warm suit which no parent could pawn; the blue-coat, which I and my wife created, resulted, oddly we thought, in internal Choir School resentment, from staff and boys. We weathered the storm.

The courtly manners of our boys endeared them to all who met them. This is no self-praise. And in performance or in choir, whether concert or service, their stillness, their dignity, their reverence, were remarked upon by all. For example, I pick out two occasions.

In the church at Chelston, Torquay (I having become separated from the party), its priest, going into the vestry, found the boys robed, sitting and silent. It gave him a shock and also material for a sermon.

On another occasion they upset the Mothers administering the ever-lavish tea by resolutely holding back from partaking, whilst the tea in the cups grew cold, until Father and Matron (my wife) had been able to arrive.

And, whether the repast was abundant or slender, a plate of cakes was left uneaten in case the hostesses should think they had not supplied enough.

Said a small boy in surprise to his father after an audition, when escorted out by a Singing Boy, "He called you *Sir*".

The manners, of course, could be at times embarrassing, as when the Head Boy rose to thank a bride (in her seventies) and a bridegroom (in his eighties) and said: "Please may we come next time?"—which brought the house down; or when surprising a Low Church Bishop by insisting on kissing his ring. It all began I know not how but grew into a tradition. If I have to hazard a suggestion it derived from our close contact with the boys of All Saints', Margaret Street, in the legendary era of Father Mackay, whose courtly manners were a vision of immortality vouchsafed in childhood.

And it came to pass that even the Ministry of Education would depart with the words: "We like your boys' manners".

## Vertu

Boys are always boys. The Eton collar, if a constraint, can never be a halo; the courtly manners can conceal mischief and even wickedness. I never had any illusions.

When a boy leaves the comparatively sheltered life of School, where "new every morning is the love", misdeeds forgiven, it is as if the incoming tide of a new life, with new faces, other minds, sweeps the past away. Perhaps, but not always, a little letter, then silence. It is so with all, it was so with me.

For instance when I was twelve I dug in my heels at home and declined to return to my Day School. My reaction, within the context of child life, was, I think, valid. Originally there was a good proportion of boys to girls; latterly the girls preponderated. I wanted and in fact needed to be in a boys' School and to that I was put. Now the point of this reminiscence is that, although my former School was within a short walk, I cannot remember going near it again to thank for the love and care bestowed on me during five long years. That had to await my penitential pilgrimage as a young priest in London to my Schoolmistress, by then retired.

The simple fact of life is that a boy can attend only to the foreground of daily life, what *has been* falls into the vaults of memory.

It is only later, as the tide of life recedes, that he finds things on the shore.

Two instances must suffice. A few years ago the Chaplain of Pentonville Prison telephoned for Palm Crosses and commented "We have one of your old boys here on a long stretch". His description left me in no doubt of identity. He was a boy—an accomplished pianist—whom I had always deeply loved and tried to help out of sticky patches of after School life. His hands had once woven Palm Crosses. Now he would be receiving one from his old School. Manners: courtly; Musick, in his time, heavenly; Vertu, alas!

*Scene:* The kitchen. Two fifteen year old boys, with co-inciding birthdays, one musical, one scholarly—good at Latin and Greek. *Weather:* One of the major freeze-ups. They have both struggled back from Kelham, frozen and famished. The musical one and the scholarly give me beatific smiles as I hand them bowls of soup. The former is now a Church Organist, the latter an overseas priest.

As we were out on a walk one day and the Angels were spotting cars the latter said: "Give me birds." He loved all natural things and taught us much.

S. KENTIGERN RESTORES THE ROBIN TO LIFE

THE CHURCH WHERE THE CHOIR SCHOOL BEGAN

St. Mary's, Seymour Street (now Eversholt Street), Somers Town, hard-by Euston Station. This is the church in the Victorian era, wherein, in the nineteen-twenties, during the post-World War I depression—its parish was one of the poorest in darkest London—what has been described as the most beautiful thing that was ever born in a slum—saw the light of day St. Mary-of-the-Angels Song School.

These pictures speak for themselves, but despite their poverty and appalling conditions, the people around (alas! not so many *in*) St. Mary's were brave and cheerful, their motto "Life ain't all yer want but it's all yer 'ave: so 'ave it. Stick a geranium in yer 'at and be 'appy." The lower picture is of Little 'ell, where police never ventured alone and the opposite side was in ruins.

A typical interior, in which the sun never entered. But the rats did.

Below—
another corner of Somers Town.

Somers Town boys, drawn by an artist of *Punch:*
"Us free go 'arves" : "There ain't goin' to be no 'arves." "Give us the core, then."
"There ain't goin' to be no core."

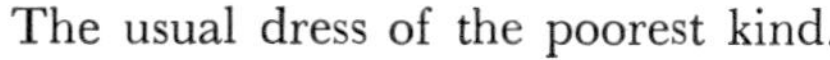

The usual dress of the poorest kind.

Typical boys of Somers Town. Always hungry and always cheerful. Father Desmond, who was very poor himself, was their Welfare State. Willie (L) became a Head boy of the Choir School. Charlie (R) became Flyweight champion of St. Pancras. We sent him to Woodbridge School. He has spent adult life in the R.A.F.

Father Desmond's annual camps, at Chailey, in Sussex, were a revelation to the boys who only knew grass as something "to keep off of". Basil Jellicoe, our Magdalen College Missioner, facilitated the camps at his home. There Father Desmond met his future wife, Marguerite Sandford, who came into camp to mend and was much afflicted by the state of his socks.

This little Charlie, who lived in "Little 'ell", was missing from the Coach, so Father Desmond went round. Charlie was undressed and in tears. So was his Mother, who had thrown a missile at him. Father Desmond won the battle, so a nice little boy held a nice piece of soap, worthy of washing the hands of (his) Pope.

"Community" grew out of the annual Camp and was cemented in a higgledy-piggledy, homely Room under the Pavement with a cupboard full of clothes and soup of the evening, after a hot wash in the sink. Everything went on at once.

Slowly, line upon line, here a little and there a little, a School began to shape.

And to that was added a Test Centre, for young men at work, who wanted to become clergy. The ending of the day was Compline. After 14 years it produced 30, one now a Canon, one a Bishop. Father Desmond tried to revive this work in 1965 but the "Establishment" said "No."

Fun in the Room under the Pavement—

"Who lifted my supper chips?"

"Who joined in?" The boy nearest Father Desmond was Henry Schumann, related to the great composer.

Our Grandmother church—Old St. Pancras. Note St. Mary's on the sky-line. Here the bell tolled at the Reformation for the last Latin Mass in London. Here the Resurrection men plied their nocturnal trade as described in *A Tale of Two Cities,* with Jerry Cruncher watching.

"A Tale of Two Pities." Father Desmond's advertisement that brought in the money to enable him to begin sending boys to a Public School, to see if slum boys could "make it". He also found the whole cost of Church re-decoration for the Centenary in 1926.

The boys we sent to Woodbridge, in their going and returning in Etons, created a School "atmosphere" in the Room under the Pavement and the preponderating non-Woodbridgeans asked if they could wear Etons on Sundays. Father Desmond appealed for grown-out-ofs, with great success.

In addition to sending boys to Woodbridge, others were enrolled in the Polytechnic and some older ones to Knutsford Test School, as having possible Vocations. Here is a homely scene with one of the Poly's.

The first Sunday was the testing time. They crept to Church in ones before the populace was up and escorted one another as a body, going home. It is difficult to see how this worked out but it is on record that there was a street scrap and they gave as good as they got, as young Church militants : surely the bravest boys anyone could wish for.

But on weekdays they dressed like this and incessantly quarrelled. It was no good giving them new clothes: if one did, the boy would disappear because his suit was pawned by his parents in their poverty. The Etons were safe, as not being pawnable.

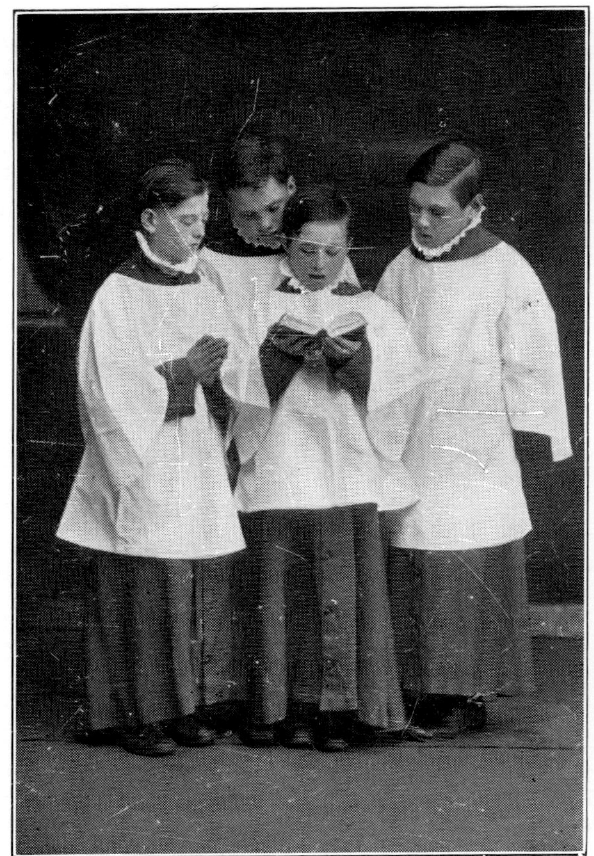

These pictures were more than propaganda—the boys used to keep Chain Prayer Saturdays—in relays.

Christmas Eve in a typical make-shift bedroom.
An authentic drawing but we doubt the pyjamas.

Came a great day in the underground room when an illuminated document was given to the boys, promising them a Choir School, but they had to wait until 1932 and older boys grew up without being able to enjoy it. But they kept faithful to St. Mary's. The Clergy, L-R, The Revds. Cecil Gault, Percy Maryon-Wilson (the new Vicar); Lord Clonmore (now the Earl of Wicklow)—obscured—next to Father Desmond, Lorimer Ries.

1931. The Lord Mayor of London, Sir William Phené Neal, lays the Foundation Stone of the still-being-built residential School in Cholmeley Park, Highgate, not far off from Dick Whittington's Stone.

The beautiful Foundation Stone of St. Mary-of-the-Angels Song School, carved by the wife of G. F. Watts, R.A.

A beginning was made as a morning Day School on 25 January 1932 in an upper room in the Magdalen College Buildings in Somers Town. On this first day Father Desmond began to realize that (a) he had given himself and his freedom as a hostage to Providence; (b) that new-made seating could collapse, as it did, and (c) there was no such thing as an unspillable ink-pot. With a community tea at 5 life went on in the Room under the Pavement until—

Note the drop-outs and the Angel-that-got-away.

The great day dawned and in the hearing of a large assembly the Bishop of London cried "Keep the Wolf from the door". A Trust had been formed with a deficit of £1,000.

This financial Albatross hung round our necks for many years.

Early days. A uniform had yet to come. But what?

Father Desmond was now in full sail upon an uncharted sea. Could he, a slum-land priest, given to homeliness, in his Room under the Pavement, become a Schoolmaster, who had to rule, and could the boys, used to the freedom of the streets, accept? It was touch and go. Remember, too, that Evensong was sung daily in Somers Town, in the vicinity of their homes, to which they went back for half-days and Sunday. Often he felt like Penelope, spinning a web only for circumstances to unravel. He made his mistakes.

Well, the uniform emerged . . . a blue smock, later called a blue-coat.

The boy nearest Father Desmond became a priest.

Somebody donated sacks of Conkers. We couldn't eat them but they made the children of Somers Town happy.

St. Mary of the Angels
v
St. Paul's Cathedral (WHITE)
1933.
*Result:* St. Paul's 3. St. Mary's 2.

Residence was kept over Christmas, for the service of the church and in the interest of the children. It should be recorded that the Song School was no tax on parish funds. It paid for everything including the Choirmaster's salary and residence. Bear this in mind as you turn the pages.

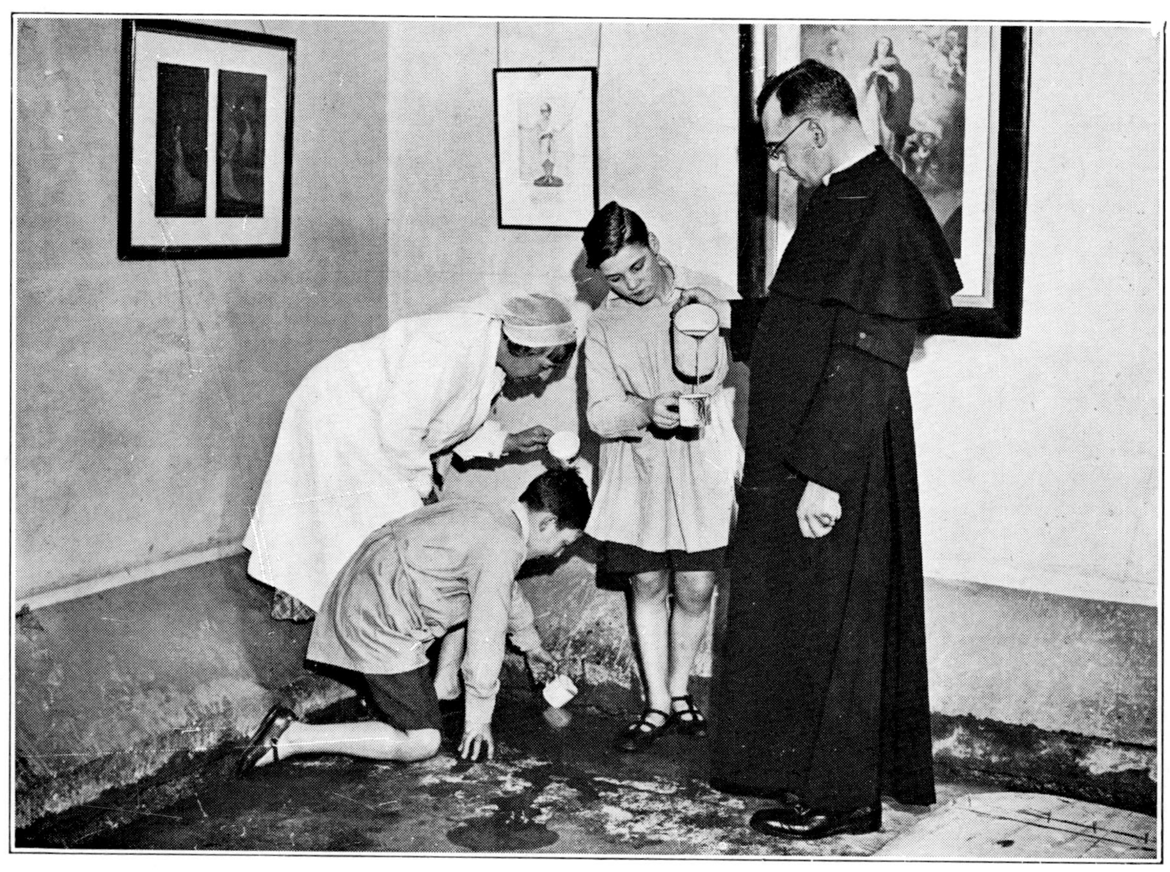

A spring of living water came up through our Refectory Floor. It was a nuisance, although good to drink.

Mr. Alfred Batts conducts an *al fresco* practice. We owe much to our Choirmasters—in sequence—Fred Kapps (a St. Mary's boy); Alfred Batts (1927-34); Conrad Lewis ('34-37); John Rollinson ('37-40); Pearce Hosken ('40-45); Conrad Lewis ('45-49); Mr. Chuckerbutty ('49-50); Prof. Clatworthy ('50-52); Robert Davies ('52-71) and, always volunteering for tours, the great Gilbert Stacey (from '52).

We staged a rather beautiful Play, called the Angelic Vision, culminating in the Everyman Theatre, Hampstead.

—inspiration came from our beautiful Grotto, with its waters.

The first winter without a fire-place in the Common Room (centrally-heated) seemed cheerless. Here the boys are singing their thanks for the Cheerful Corner given them.

Jean Stirling Mackinlay hired the Angels for her Christmas Plays. The tallest boy is the one who split to Father Desmond about the Plot to put sneezing powder into the Dragon's jaws.

On Christmas Eve we used to go down to the Embankment and serve the Down-and-outs; then invite them to a Boxing-day dinner at Highgate. More pictures follow.

This is an artist's conception of our Down-and-outs' Party and true to the event. He put the white blobs on the Pudding for donors to record their gifts.

Father Desmond celebrates. The Christmas hospitality included bed and breakfast tickets in a Hostel.

Roy Michael Lewys. (R.I.P.)
Accidentally killed when on War leave.

David Copperfield's home in Johnson Street, restored as a Children's Library by the Revd. John Brett Langstaff, Magdalen College Missioner. He was succeeded by Basil Jellicoe, in the early 'twenties. This historic building was destroyed by the St. Pancras Authority when re-building.

Christmas for the homeless at Highgate.

Maurice, early days and after. He was awarded *La Croix de Guerre* by France.

George, who landed in France on D-Day, dug a trench and conducted night prayers. Hymn : Bless this House.

Mary Morse-Boycott, in her ballet dress, at the age of 14, in the Song School Garden.

Father Desmond was a front rank exponent of the Art of Diabolo but spurned the craze of Yo-Yo.

A Septuagesima Custom. Whipping out the Alleluia Top. "Sing Alleluia forth with duteous praise . . ."

About 1933, to Father Desmond's distress, his Room under the Pavement, which he needed as his Somers Town Centre for his Mothers, recruitment of boys and enjoyment of the resident Song School boys during holiday breaks, was taken away from him, in favour of other parochial purposes. In the empty room he knelt and wept. He and his wife bought a house over a paper shop to replace it, but it turned to their loss. Before he could open it his work *in* Somers Town, although not *for* it, came to a shocking and unnecessary end.

The old clergy group was dissolving: John Hampden Thompson (Vicar); Basil Jellicoe (Magdalen College Mission); Fathers Desmond and Will Wynne.

It was basically due to the wish of a large staff to establish the principle of celibacy. The first thing a principle does is to kill someone—or thing

Father Desmond had worked without stipend from 1924; covered all School and Choir expenses; in 1926 had raised the money for Church restoration; always submitted to the new Vicar his appeals before publication and can say (with his hand on his heart) was a loyal subordinate, and could not believe it when a colleague came down one night into his Room under the Pavement to warn him (whether as friend or emissary he does not know) that "the Vicar is going to get rid of you." He could not believe it because the Vicar was his dearest friend. But so it came to pass. The Chairman of the Trust (Canon Dudley Symon) put the blame entirely on the parish clergy. This is history.

On Candlemas Sunday 1935 the Angels sang for the last time in St. Mary's, not any more wanted. A bewildered Father Desmond gathered up at midnight the needed equipment of the Song School. His choir of old boys were urged to carry on. The reasons for this heart-breaking and by him undesired rupture have been dwelt upon in his *A Tapestry of Toil.*

Under the inspiration and heroic labours of Basil Jellicoe, whose funeral the Song School was to sing in Chailey Church, Sussex, slum tenements were being replaced by model dwellings.

Thus a light (so needlessly) quenched in Somers Town shone upon the Church at large. The Song School embarked on tours wherever a door was opened. Would the Church Established adopt and foster it as its own Mobile-Music-Squad? It had nothing to lose—only a Handmaid to gain.

Crossing the River Mersey.

# Les petits chanteurs de Sainte-Marie des Anges

*Fondateur de l'Ecole de Sainte-Marie des Anges, le Rév. Desmond Morse-Boycott est également connu comme écrivain et journaliste. Aidé de sa femme, il entreprit sa belle œuvre il y a quelques années. Ses premiers petits élèves reçurent le gîte et l'instruction dans une modeste chambre située au sous-sol d'un pauvre immeuble londonien. Fruit d'un labeur acharné et d'une persévérance à toute épreuve, s'élève aujourd'hui un magnifique collège. Les enfants qui y entrent pauvres en ressortent riches d'un bien que personne ne leur pourra ravir: la foi et l'instruction.*

Sans la Radio, nous n'aurions peut-être pas eu le privilège d'entendre ces jeunes gas d'Outre-Manche, venus en Suisse en tournée de propagande.

On se souvient de leurs claires voix entonnant des chants religieux anciens, des hymnes anglais, tout un répertoire varié exécuté sans musique avec une conviction et une sérénité sans égale.

L'interview du Rév. Desmond Morse-Boycott est un peu décousue et pour cause... Elle a lieu dans le car qui transporte les petits chanteurs de La Sallaz à la gare de Lausanne. La pluie gifle les vitres derrière lesquelles nos gentils hôtes n'aperçoivent de la capitale vaudoise que la route glissante et les arbres en pleurs!

— Que pensez-vous de la Suisse?

— Qu'elle ne change pas beaucoup de Londres, répond avec humour le Révérend, en montrant le temps.

Mais aussitôt, il témoigne sa sympathie pour notre pays qu'il a choisi comme premier but de son voyage sur le Continent. Les élèves de Sainte-Marie des Anges n'avaient encore jamais quitté l'Angleterre. Il a pensé que la Suisse leur réserverait bon accueil pour deux raisons: la première parce que, étant un pays de verdure où niche à profusion une gent ailée et musicienne, ses jeunes «oiseaux» chanteurs s'y trouveraient à l'aise; la seconde à cause de sa population réputée très musicienne qui apprécierait peut-être leurs concerts.

Qui penserait, en les voyant, que ces garçons sont tous des enfants de parents pauvres, très pauvres? insiste le Révérend. Vêtus du charmant costume de leur collège, ils ont l'apparence d'élèves d'un riche institut anglais: pantalons bleu marine, manteau et béret de même teinte, blouse bleu clair et gland de ton semblable sur le béret. Au collège, ils revêtent le pantalon long, la blouse blanche garnie d'un col rouge.

*Ce jeune garçon aux yeux malicieux dans un visage expressif se nomme Stephen Morgan. Solo des chanteurs de Sainte-Marie des Anges, il est âgé de 13 ans. Son père est chauffeur de taxi à Londres. La limpide voix de Stephen Morgan a conquis jusqu'au Négus qui a fait don à l'enfant d'un petit anneau d'or qu'il porte à l'annulaire droit.*

Leur visage témoigne d'une existence exempte de soucis. A part la musique qui est la base de leur instruction, ils étudient les langues vivantes et les langues mortes ainsi que les branches pour lesquelles ils ont le plus d'aptitudes; ils pratiquent les sports et sortent de Sainte-Marie des Anges armés pour la vie. Ces enfants n'ont pas l'impression pénible d'être dépendants de la charité publique; ils subviennent à leurs besoins en donnant des concerts. Ils ont chanté à l'église anglaise de Lausanne, Genève et Montreux. La B. B. C. ne les ayant jamais autorisé à donner d'auditions, c'est à Lausanne qu'ils connurent pour la première fois les émotions du micro!

— Bonne chance, gentils chanteurs! Et merci!

Alors, en guise d'adieu, avec un sourire grand «comme ça», le jeune solo répond en français, en cherchant ses mots:

— Il n'y a pas de quoi! C. G.

*A gauche: Fred Brazier, 14 ans, dirige ses petits camarades avec le sérieux et la conscience d'un vieux chef d'orchestre. Les voix jaillissent souples et obéissantes sous la conduite du geste qui modèle les inflections.*

*Chanter, chanter encore, dans les églises, les salles de concert, en plein air, c'est de la joie qui éclate avec toute la conviction de la jeunesse.*
*(Photos Fred Schmid)*

*A droite: Déjà il faut quitter Lausanne. Les petits choristes se dirigent vers le grand hall de la gare où, avant de partir, ils donnent un dernier concert aussi apprécié qu'inattendu.*

From *La Semaine,* to whom we are indebted for pictures. Note incorrect caption to circular picture. For Fred Brazier read Arthur Hoare.

Father Desmond had, all along, down along, out along lea, to combat the (then) Board of Education and local Authorities, who disapproved of the Tours, and regarded Music as a subtraction from General Education, which, during our wanderings, was never neglected.

Meanwhile our Test Centre, for working men to help them to become priests, continued into the early days of the war.

What do we do now? John Cornelius (L.) and Geoffrey Jenkins (R.) hold the Choir School in their hands, all four bags of it.

I wonder what we have to do tomorrow?

Singing "Lead, Kindly Light" outside Newman's Cottages at Littlemore, Oxford: on the centenary occasion.

The Angels meet the Vienna Song School boys. The *News Chronicle* organized a performance by us to follow theirs, to show that English boys could do as well, and they did.

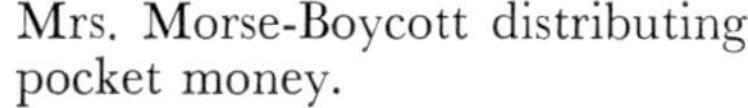

Mrs. Morse-Boycott distributing pocket money.

*Les Petits Chanteurs à la Croix de Bois* welcome *Les Rossignols* (the Nightingales).

Our boy with the Golden Voice was Stephen Morgan. We had to give them what they called "little bonnet" as a souvenir.

FORM I [7-10]

David. J. Bailay
D Ian Pain
John Scott
Basil Kalaher
Joseph T. How
Charles Jobbins.
Samuel. R. Bugg.
Maurice Hobbins

FORM II [11-plus]

Thomas Connor.
Cyril J. Emery.
William H. Palmer.
Victor J. Shennan.
Arthur, L, Pither,
Roy W. Lewys.

FORM III [13 plus]

Gordon S. Rolland
Rex Viner.
Maurice Rosson
William Price
Robert Hoare
Leonard Maycock.
Leonard. Golding.
John Eagleton

The signatures of the first residential Singing Boys—in 1932. Contrast them if you can bear it—with those of the modern boy.

In 1938 the School moved to a spacious estate at Addlestone, near Weybridge, Surrey, with the approval of its Trustees. Sale of the Highgate premises to the L.C.C. put the School on to a sounder financial basis, allowed for expansion and eased the acute problem of nearness to the Church that welcomed us no longer. Besides, the threat of war and consequent dispersal darkened the sky. But no one regretted this more at the time than Father Desmond: if the School had remained until the great evacuation it would have "folded up". The premises suffered from damage in the blitz. The new estate provided a playing field, which was a great attraction . . . a paddock, greenhouses, a vinery, an orchard and outbuildings.

The new School on Woburn Hill, Addlestone. We began to plan the addition of a wing.

Marguerite Morse-Boycott and her boy commies, David and Patrick.

Came Wistaria time.

Came Logging Time.

Came Pagan Time, came Bushing an unpopular boy.

Came always the Home letter. Fine handwriting and matters of interest were insisted upon. You don't get that from boys today.

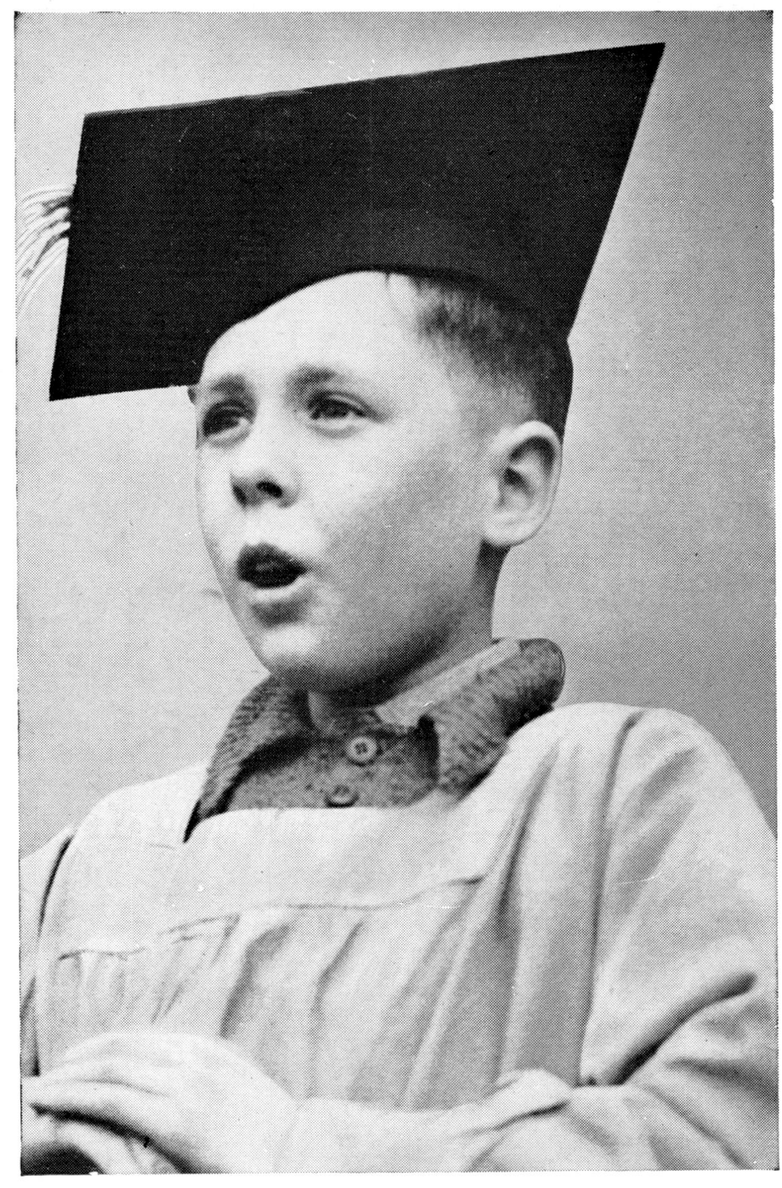

Allan Keith Jones, of Rushall, near Walsall, on his first tour.

Came an April day when new drainage up a long drive meant no water for awhile, so Father Desmond organized a tour of Devon and off we all did go, but alas! Within 48 hours the School was burnt to the ground. We have never found out how it happened. And there was no water! That was in 1940.

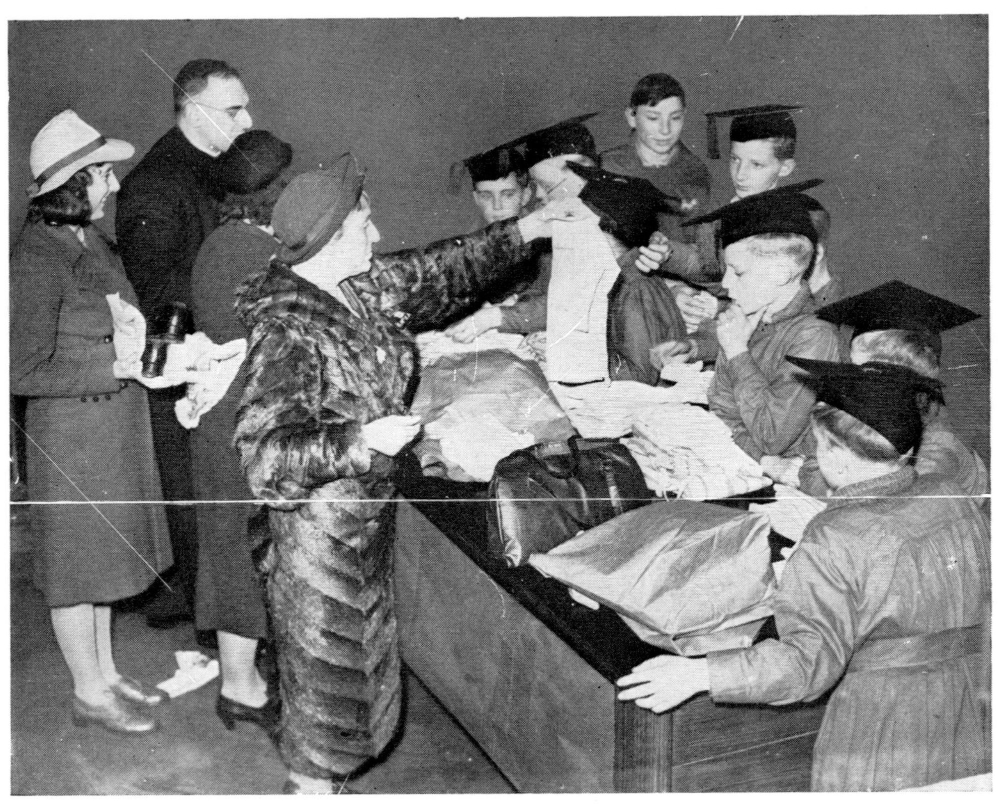

Two weeks later we met the boys returning from the Tour, on Paddington Station, with remnants of kit from the Laundry.

Two months later—singing Evensong on the ruins.

George Helsdon, a Somers Town boy, from early age one of Father Desmond's handfuls. In later life George told him the following: "I was sitting in your study when you came up to me, and said, 'One day you will be a priest'." George was sent, at 13, to Woodbridge School: he came down at 17, unsettled, and parted from us. He came back, during the war, a Roman Catholic priest—a saintly and charming character. He died comparatively young, sending a message of thanks and love. R.I.P.

At the time of the fire a house named Amroth, contiguous to our estate (Woburn Chase), fell vacant: we secured a year's lease and piled in. Here are Cyril and Patrick employed as you see.

School life began again under daily improvisation.

The boy painting is Maris, whom we later sent to the T.S. *Mercury*.

This an interlude to (a) cheer you up and (b) inform you that the Song School was the first to make a chink in the Iron Curtain between Canterbury and Rome by becoming—

The only Anglican Choir School to be honoured by membership of the International Society of Little Singers.

From things that go bang in the night—
Good Lord deliver us.

Peter (now an Organist)

As the Doodle-bugs swept over us nightly we took refuge in a Coal Cellar. The Siren began at 6 p.m. and ended twelve hours later.

War-time Rations—hence the hungry expectancy.
No "modern boys" fads then! They would eat anything except canned Snoek—could anyone with a name like that!

Choirmaster Pearce Hosken—a great master of Plainchant.

Because we had begun to dig the Foundations of a Wing onto the destroyed House, one week before the outbreak of War, we were allowed to continue and here is the result.

Leonard meets the Talking Doll. You can spot Leonard because he wears specs.

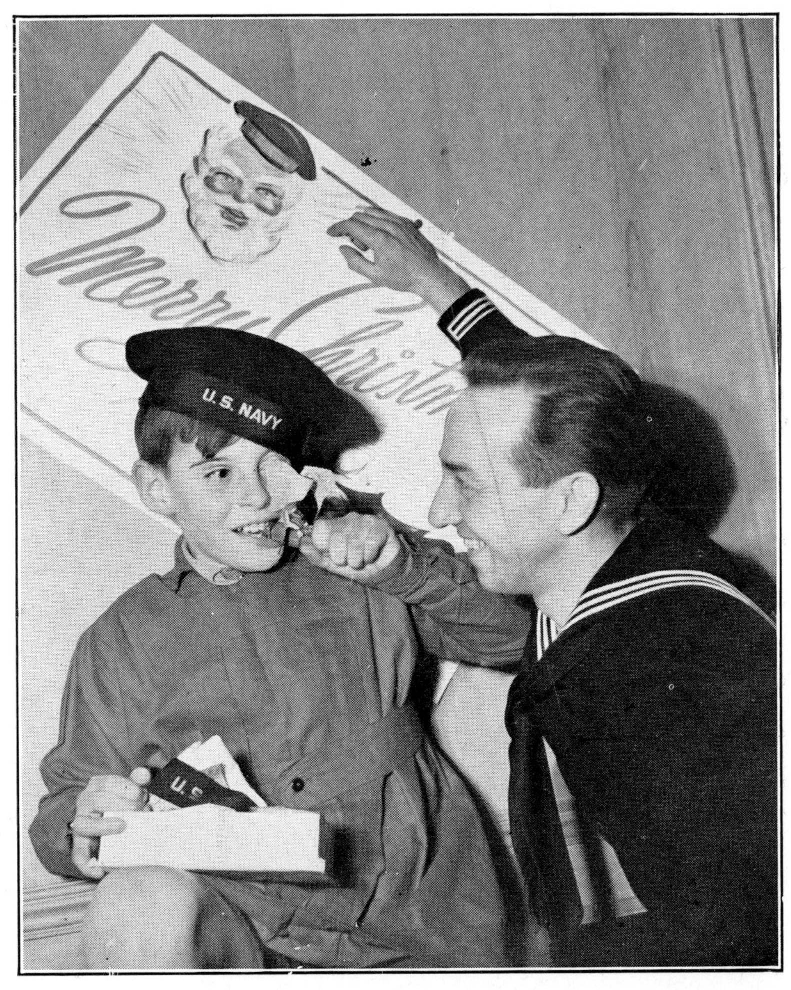


Meanwhile, we went around singing, entertaining troops, and had residential interludes in Devon.

But always the next meal, on rations, and the Mother of the School seldom failed to meet emergencies. One day the Refectory was engulphed (Ruskin's spelling) in silence as we nibbled at Pease-soup. Then Miss Morse-Boycott cried out "It's been made from my Pigeons' Food. And it's expensive!" We all stopped eating, thankfully, with the exception of one, who said: "It's good!" The Cook was to blame.

And here is Mrs. Morse-Boycott, so thankful that dinner has gone off successfully, that she gets on with embroidery for sale.

Mrs. Morse-Boycott and daughter Mary shared all the disturbances and distress of the times. This included our being put out on the doorstep of our evacuation home at Lee on Sea, North Devon, at Noon on 1 January 1942. The landlord refused a temporary extension of lease. We took refuge in Exmouth.

But by that Summer we were back in Addlestone, in the new-built wing, and on the direct line of the Doodle-bugs. One night we had a V2 explode in our vicinity. It broke a mustard pot.

Scripting in Father Desmond's Study on a Sunday afternoon.

An Art Class in progress.
As you see, Winston Churchill (Father Desmond's cousin) was the victim of his brush.

His first effort at portraiture began, as you can see, from his easel on the left. Here is the result.

Staffing difficulty was acute and Do-it-yourself was often the order of the day.

Philomel, the Song School Goat.

The Tiddlers' Sand-pit.

It is difficult to keep in touch with old boys and to know how they have faced up to the Battle of Life, but Allan (extreme Left) became a young expert Shorthand writer before leaving us to go into the Timber Trade, and John (extreme Right) is now a rising musician.

The Beating of Bounds: Ascension Day, 1950. 8 years beat 7 years. Each boy watches with unholy glee . . . till his turn comes.

The Calf is not as happy as Michael, who is now a Schoolmaster.

Father Desmond, followed by Gilbert Stacey, our great Musician-Patron, in the communal Procession to the Olive Tree, in Menton, *c.* 1950. We can't remember, now, what it was all about. We toured the Riviera for three wonderful weeks, singing in churches, hotels, and on the bandstand.

Oh! for the sound of the tea-bell . . .

Silver Wedding celebration.

A time to gain and a time to lose and it's time for chapel now. L.-R.: William Browne, Edward Hallewell, Martin Froggatt and David Crocker.

John Salt, who had a lovely voice, was a good Pupil Teacher. His "Alleluia" by Mozart was incomparably recorded by the Song School shortly after H.M.V. had dismissed him for voice-break. How wrong can experts be!

Musical Reflections.

Father Desmond's Painting for the Song School's Silver Jubilee. Every brick was painted separately.

Michael in somewhat mis-fitting Etons but proud to wear them.

In 1952, owing to our inability to discharge a Mortgage after the death of a great Benefactor, whose Executors claimed cash, we had to sell the Addlestone estate and re-settle, to "make do and mend", at Three Gables in Beaconsfield, the only home we could find in eight weeks of desperate searching. The picture shows Mrs. Morse-Boycott beginning on the garden.

Preparation for the daily morning prayer: "Shower down thy blessings, O Lord".

Father Desmond scrubbing . . .

The Evangelists are now in the Garden of Walnut Tree Cottage.

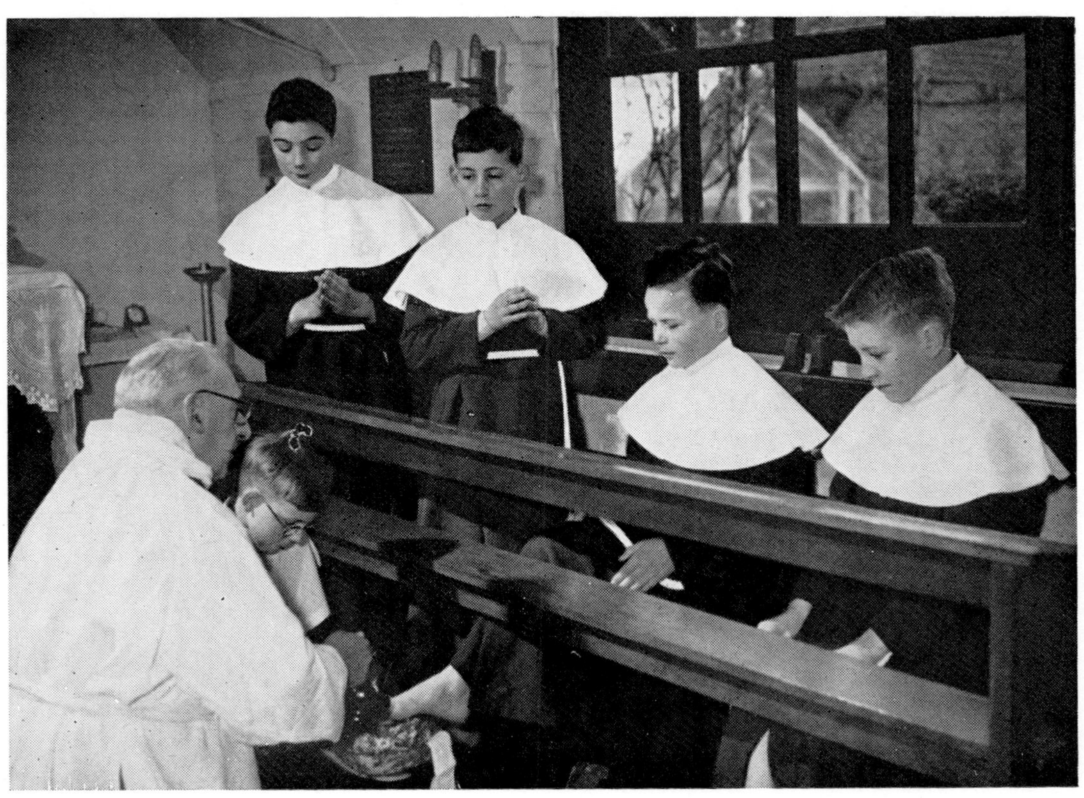

Maundy Thursday.

Games in the Garden: Christopher, with Club, went into the Navy. Anthony (bending over) is a priest. Gordon (o'ertopping) is a Craftsman and Scoutmaster.

Television at Christmas in St. Martin-in-the-Fields. As an historical fact our boys were the first ever to be on T.V. in the old Ally Pally—under Mr. Cecil Madden, early pioneer.

The joy of a boy when the National Playing Fields' Association made the above donation.

The revered Mother of the Song School was a firm disciplinarian with a tender heart. The boys had a saying : "Out with Father, in with Matron". And *vice versa.* Of course, we worked it that way. Scene—Chailey, Sussex.

During 1959, East-end boys under their leader, Mr. Bill Kishkey, kept our tradition alive. Here they are, servicing a Wedding. We called them Teddy-Angels. P.T.O.

The Teddy-angels (see p. 83) were non-resident boys—the School having had to close under a 1958 Credit Squeeze and lacking funds and work. The "Establishment" was deaf to our appeals.

In January, 1960, Father Desmond re-commenced the residential School with a few little boys gathered out of nowhere, restless as rabbits in straw and with voices like penny whistles. A new era dawned . . .

Before the ending of the day.

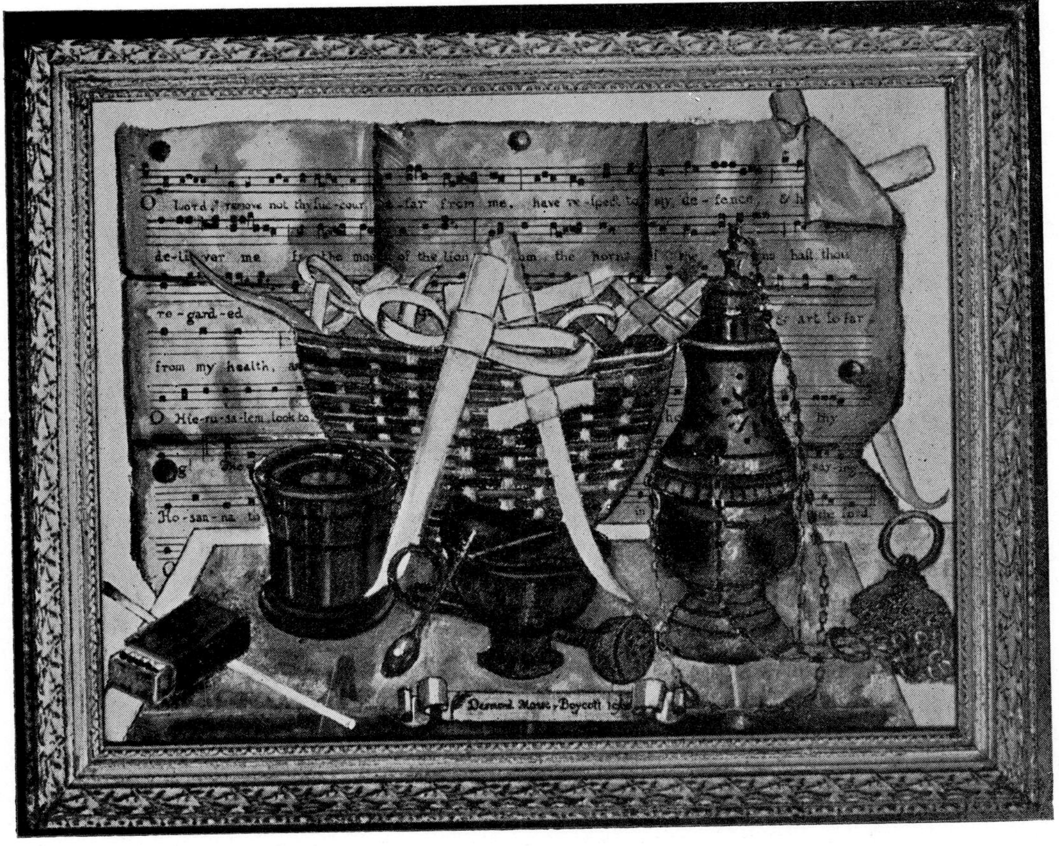


Palm Sunday Array. A painting by Father Desmond.

*Unsolicited Award:*
This
Certificate of Merit
proclaimed throughout the World
is awarded to
Desmond Lionel Morse-Boycott
for DISTINGUISHED SERVICE
to Church Music and Art
and is the subject of notice in the
*Dictionary of International Biography*
11 September 1967

Father Desmond and his "instrument of ten strings", as says the Psalmist.

Our Palm Cross weaving industry is a major source of income. 30,000 crosses and 250 supporting churches are our tally.

S.M.d.A = Sainte Marie des Anges = Santa Maria degli Angels: and the Dicky Bird the original Cockney Sparrow.

**BEHOLD**

The disappointed cleric who hoped for a copy of Father Desmond's richly illustrated Autobiography

A TAPESTRY OF TOIL:

£2·50 plus 16p postage. But he can have one from Faith Press, Wing Road, Leighton Buzzard, LU7 7NQ, or from the Revd. Desmond Morse-Boycott: Founder and Administrator of the St. Mary-of-the-Angels Song School Trust: Walnut Tree Cottage, 79 Ashacre Lane, Offington, Worthing, Sussex: Telephone 60927.

Copies from the Author carry Autographed Bookplate.

The book is as full of wisdom as fun and foolishness, for a Church that's forgotten to laugh. Be wise and buy now.

The ideal gift to your priest.

## BOY BISHOPS

BY the Middle Ages the Boy Bishop ceremony had gained such a hold on the affections of young and old that all Cathedrals and Collegiate churches had a Boy Bishop annually. Two reasons seem to have made it so popular: the mediaeval love of Mystery Plays and the desire to impress on children the honour and dignity of Holy Orders.

Nowadays the ceremony needs adaptation, and the Revd. Desmond Morse-Boycott has "created" a rite, which may be used with his permission by any parish, with local adaptation.[1]

Despite the above, whilst enthroning a Boy Bishop with all due reverence, and making an offering of a piece of money (in the case of St. Mary-of-the-Angels Song School a guinea), the "consecrator" no doubt reserves the right, should occasion arise, to lay the Boy Bishop across the school bench and say, "My Lord, this is going to hurt you more than it hurts me". It is a remarkable fact, however, that so highly is the position prized by a Choir School Boy, and so reverently and seriously undertaken, that it has the effect of producing exemplary School conduct for the period in question. Incidentally, there is no attempt to ordain or consecrate the Boy Bishop in the episcopal sense of ordination or consecration, and to make this plain the term "sealing" was chosen in St. Mary-of-the-Angels Song School.

The Boy Bishop is elected by his fellow-scholars on December 5th, the Eve of St. Nicholas' Day, and if he is willing to accept the privilege of office should make his confession and receive Holy Communion prior to his Sealing on the Day, which ceremony may be done in public in a church (preferably one dedicated to St. Nicholas) or in the privacy of the School chapel, as serves convenience. He then holds office until Holy Innocents' Day, December 28th, when his beautiful robes are ceremoniously laid aside in a simple ceremony—"wipping out".

What are the necessary qualifications for office? Exemplary conduct? Hardly so. The ceremony is the Sealing of a Prince of the scholars, not of a prig. A good deal of discretion has, however, to be used for it would never do to have a Boy Bishop who might fall into a serious scrape at any time. However, the Principal and his staff discuss the matter carefully and nominate or suggest certain boys as having stability of character. That done, there is a secret ballot, and the "runner up" will be given the position of Chaplain, with an emolument of half-a-guinea. He must attend on the Boy Bishop continually, fetch his robes, carry his crozier, etc. A second qualification is the possession of a good voice for chanting the services. As that rules out new boys and boys with changing voices, the boy is usually in the middle form of the School. A third qualification, of a domestic sort at that, as a Choir School cannot have a new set of magnifical robes every year, is that the boy must fit the robes. If he is too small, he must wait until he fits.

[1] *The Boy Bishop Book.* An illustrated historical and liturgical monograph, autographed. Obtainable from the Author for 50 pence.

The first Chylde Bishop since the Reformation.
✠ Frederick St. Mary-of-the-Angels blesses his class-mates.

*Special Note*

I HAVE a rare, perhaps unique, book entitled *The Antiquities of Sarum,* published in 1771, in whose leaves there has been bound a pamphlet called "Episcopus Puerorum", published in 1683. The former took cognizance of the latter, and in a chapter on the Choral Bishop asserts that "In the Cathedral of Sarum is a Monument in Stone of a Boy habited in Episcopal Robes, Mitre on his head, and a Crozier in his hand. It lay long buried under the seats near the Pulpit, but on the removal of the latter, about the year 1680, it was discovered, and removed to the North part of the Nave; where at first it was covered with a wooden box." Curiosity demolished this, and then Mr. John Gregory, the Bishop's chaplain, "took a good deal of pains in inquiring into the origin of so extraordinary a Monument". "It now lieth", he says, "betwixt the Pillars, covered over with a Box of Wood, not without a general imputation of Rarity and Reverence, it seeming almost impossible to everyone, that either a *Bishop* could be so small in *Person,* or a *Child* so great in *Cloaths*".

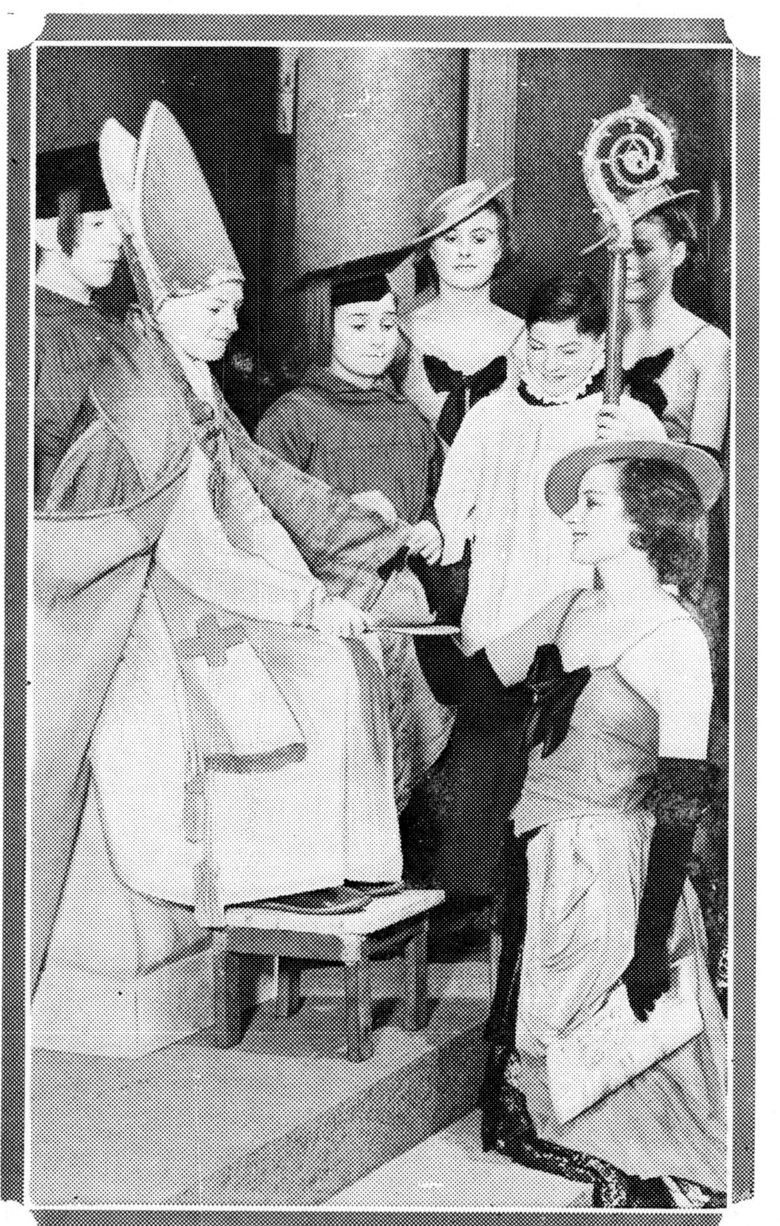

The first Chylde Bishop is welcomed by the legitimate Stage and "condescends" to receive a bag of money for his "Diocese", which later on he transmits to Father Desmond.

How to deal with the Establishment.

Alas! on Holy Innocents' Day he is obliged to disrobe and, clothed in sackcloth, submit to being "wipped" out of Office and pensioned off with his guinea. Theoretically he has "forty stripes save one" to tally with the xxxix Articles.

The second Chylde Bishop : ✠ Maurice St. Mary-of-the-Angels.

The priest nominates the Chylde Bishop and if there is more than one candidate the boys vote. The ballot is secret.

The Presentation and Interrogation.

Singing Boys impose their right hands in the Sealing.

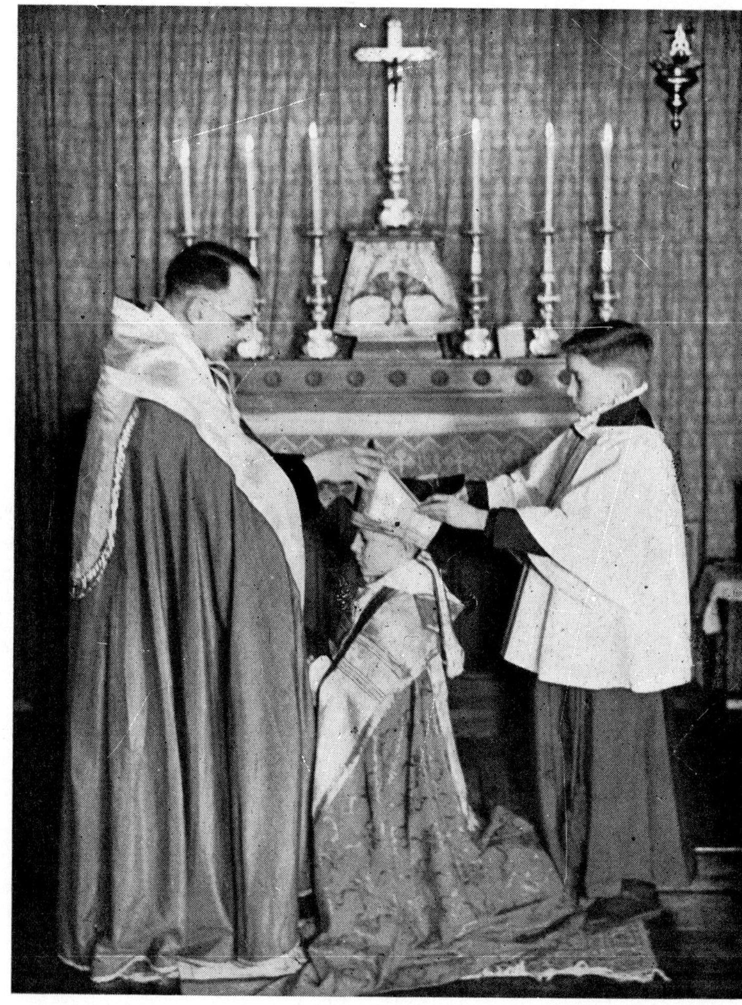

The robing.

The Tribute Money.

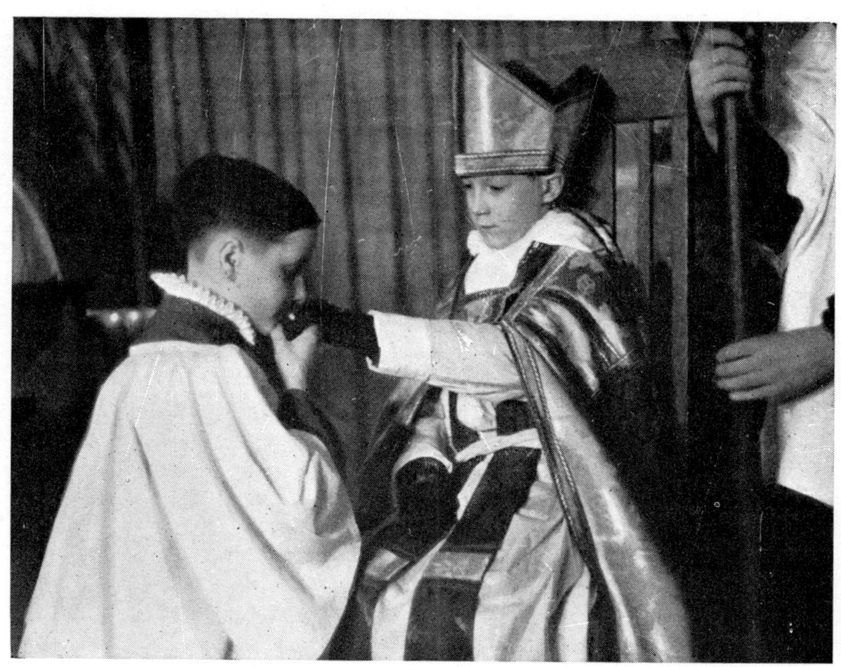

Homage : David, kissing the ring, grew up into Anglican Holy Orders, then Roman. Father Desmond christened him at one month, received him at seven years, kept him until he was seventeen.

✠ Mervyn St. Mary-of-the Angels blessing the incense.

✠ Noel. Note the carved Throne, on the back of which all the names of Chylde-Bishops are engraved.

Now let old and young uniting Chant to thee harmonious lays, Boys and girls together singing With pure heart their song of praise,

*Evermore and evermore.*

✠ David St. Mary-of-the-Angels.

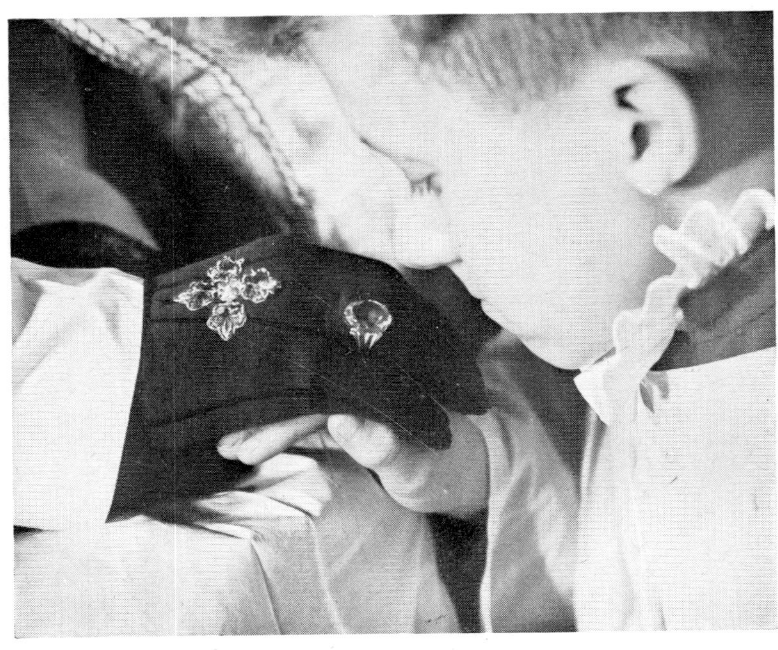

Vincent Baker kisses the Boy Bishop's ring.

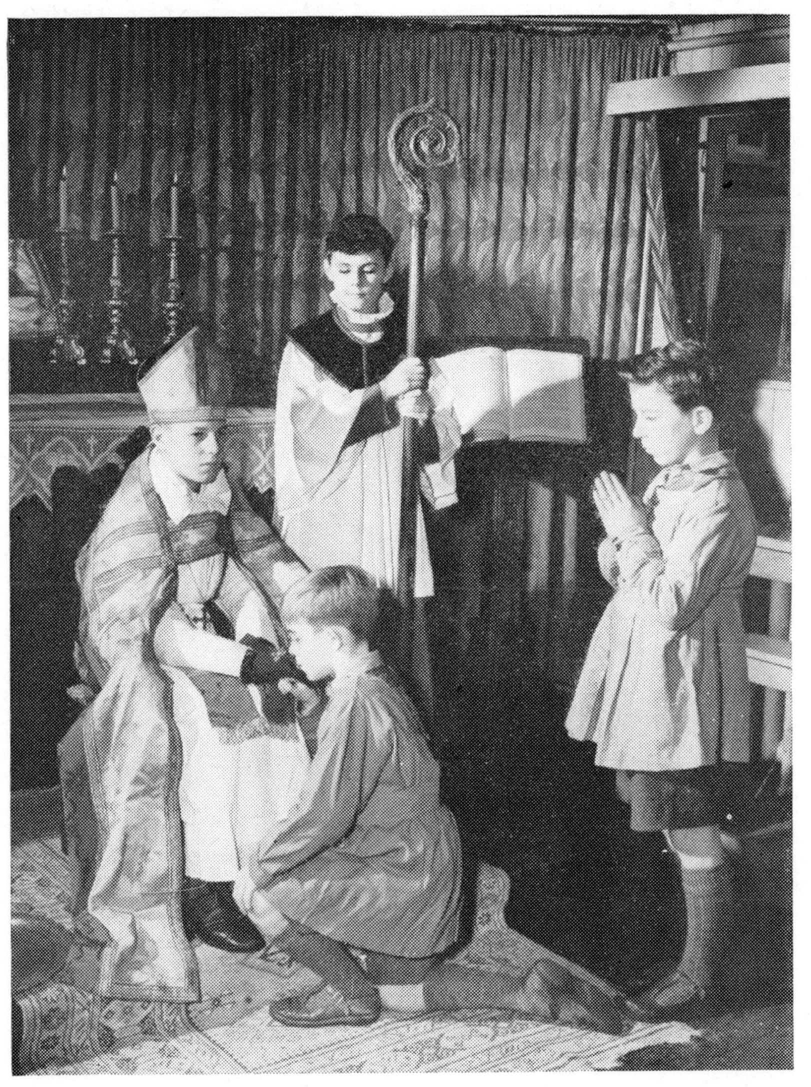

✠ Anthony St. Mary-of-the-Angels.
Attendant boys L-R Martin Froggatt, John Steer (chaplain), Michael Dewi Parry.

✠ Peter St. Mary-of-the-Angels—son of a priest.
Now a Doctor.

Before the School was burnt down. This makes us think of a gold fish tank. It was the oval window in Father's study. Beneath "Pennies from Heaven."

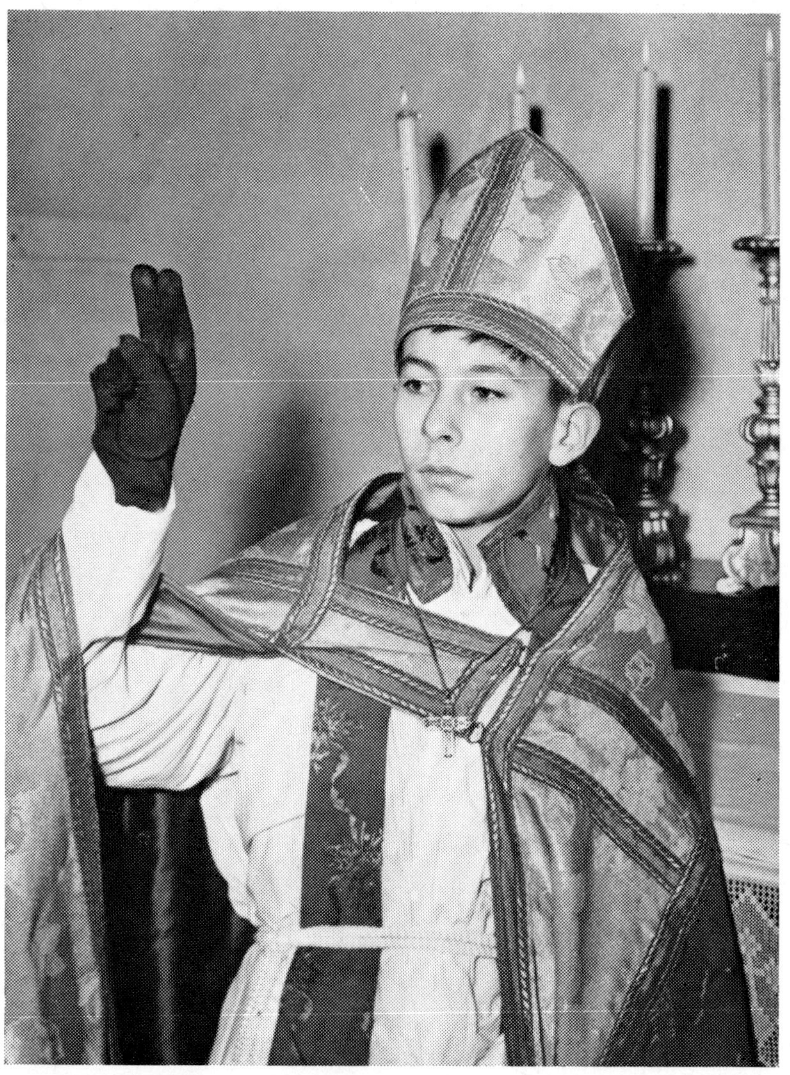

✠ Anthony St. Mary-of-the-Angels, now a priest, with a Parish in New Zealand. Trained by Kelham.

✠ Timothy St. Mary-of-the-Angels. He gained a Scholarship at Ellesmere. Anthony Ward and Stuart Mount attend.

Myself when young.

Please carry my work into the future
by gifts and legacies.

Solicitors to the Trust—Riders, 8 New Square, Lincoln's Inn, London, WC2A 3QP, who will supply information. Donations to Barclays Bank, Addlestone, Surrey, or to me. Address: Walnut Tree Cottage, 79 Ashacre Lane, Offington, Worthing, Sussex, England. 60927.

Iesu mercy
I am small and of no
reputation, yet do I not
forget thy commandments.